Zoom In on Amazing Authors

Charles Schulz

Jennifer Strand

abdopublishing.com

Published by Abdo Zoom™, PO Box 398166, Minneapolis, Minnesota 55439. Copyright © 2017 by Abdo Consulting Group, Inc. International copyrights reserved in all countries. No part of this book may be reproduced in any form without written permission from the publisher. Abdo Zoom™ is a trademark and logo of Abdo Consulting Group, Inc.

Printed in the United States of America, North Mankato, Minnesota
062016
092016

THIS BOOK CONTAINS RECYCLED MATERIALS

Cover Photo: Douglas Kirkland/Corbis
Interior Photos: Douglas Kirkland/Corbis, 1; AP Images, 4, 18; Shutterstock Images, 5, 14; iStockphoto, 6–7, 9; Seth Poppel/Yearbook Library, 8; Rodrigo Reyes Marin/AFLO/AP Images, 11, 19; Randall Benton/Sacramento Bee/MCT via Getty Images, 12; Walter Daran/The LIFE Images Collection/Getty Images, 13; ABC Photo Archives/© ABC/Getty Images, 15, 19; 20th Century Fox/PA Wire URN:25048603/AP Images, 16–17

Editor: Emily Temple
Series Designer: Madeline Berger
Art Direction: Dorothy Toth

Publisher's Cataloging-in-Publication Data
Names: Strand, Jennifer, author.
Title: Charles Schulz / by Jennifer Strand.
Description: Minneapolis, MN : Abdo Zoom, [2017] | Series: Amazing authors | Includes bibliographical references and index.
Identifiers: LCCN 2016941363 | ISBN 9781680792133 (lib. bdg.) |
    ISBN 9781680793819 (ebook) | 9781680794700 (Read-to-me ebook)
Subjects: LCSH: Schulz, Charles M.--Juvenile literature. | Cartoonists--United
    States--Biography--Juvenile literature.
Classification: DDC 741.5/092 [B]--dc23
LC record available at http://lccn.loc.gov/2016941363

Table of Contents

Introduction 4

Early Life 6

Rise to Fame 10

Career 12

Legacy. 16

Quick Stats 20

Key Dates 21

Glossary 22

Booklinks 23

Index 24

Introduction

Charles Schulz was a **cartoonist**. He created the *Peanuts* **comic strip**.

It includes famous **characters** Charlie Brown and Snoopy.

5

Early Life

Charles was born on November 26, 1922.

He lived in Minnesota. He loved comic strips. He liked drawing his favorite characters.

Charles had a hard time in school.

But he took a **correspondence course**. He learned to make comic strips.

Rise to Fame

Schulz made a comic strip for a newspaper. It was called *Li'l Folks*. The characters were kids.

But they had grown-up thoughts.

Career

Schulz wanted more newspapers to run his comic. He sent out samples.

Soon he got his wish.

The strip was renamed *Peanuts*. The characters became **popular**.

Many newspapers added the comic.

Legacy

Schulz made the *Peanuts* comic strip for 50 years.

Peanuts was turned into movies and TV specials. It was also a musical play.

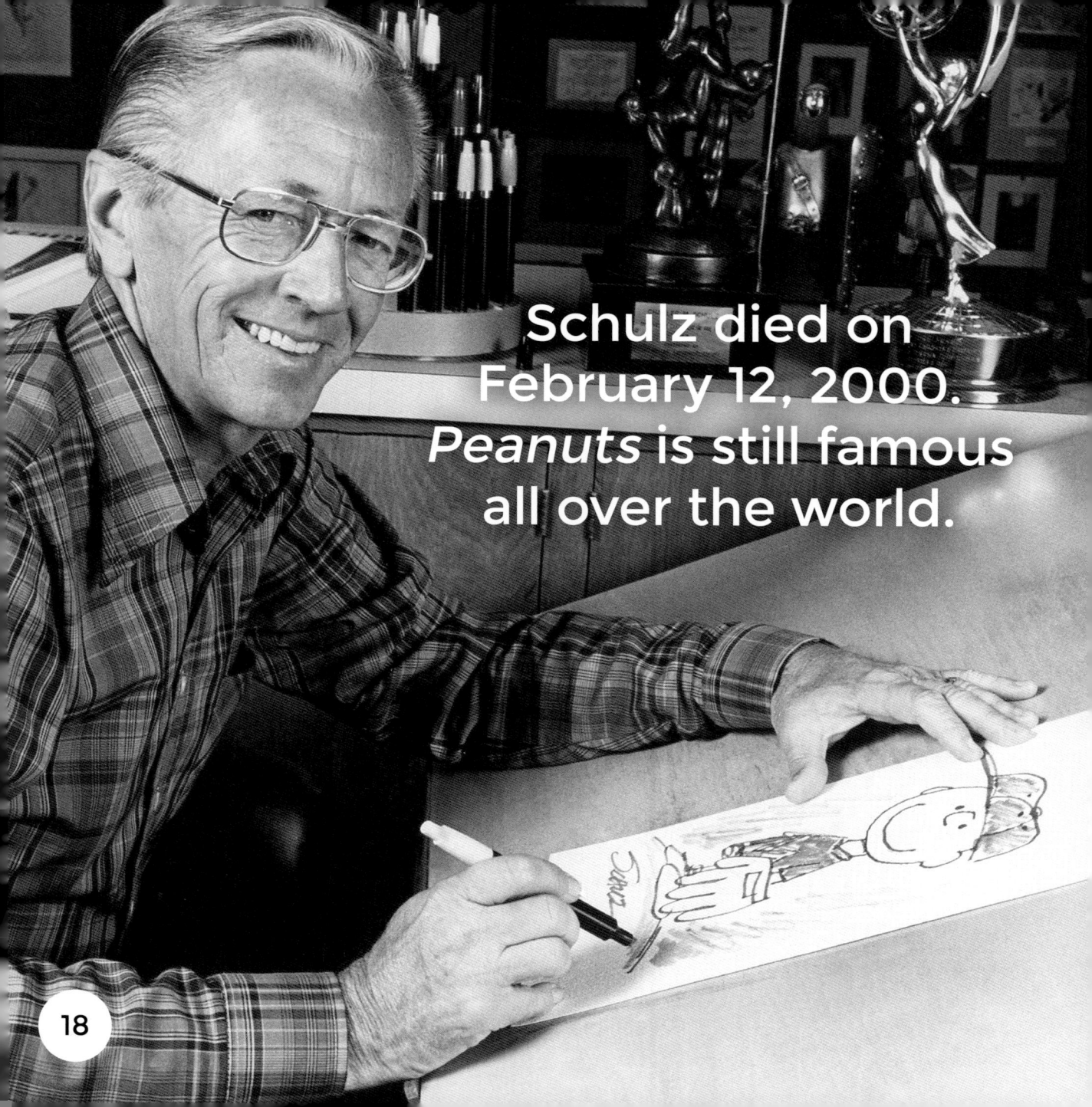

Schulz died on February 12, 2000. *Peanuts* is still famous all over the world.

Millions of people love the characters.

Quick Stats

Charles Schulz

Born: November 26, 1922

Birthplace: Minneapolis, Minnesota

Wives: Joyce Halverson (divorced); Jeannie Forsyth

Known For: Schulz created the *Peanuts* comic strip.

Died: February 12, 2000

Key Dates

1922: Charles Monroe Schulz is born on November 26.

1943-1945: Schulz serves in the US Army during World War II.

1947: *Li'l Folks* is first published in a newspaper.

1950: The comic strip is renamed *Peanuts*.

1965: *A Charlie Brown Christmas* is the first *Peanuts* TV special.

2000: Schulz dies on February 12.

Glossary

cartoonist - someone who draws funny pictures, such as in a comic strip.

characters - people in a story.

comic strip - a story told in a series of drawings.

correspondence course - a class given by mail instead of in a classroom.

popular - liked or enjoyed by many people.

Booklinks

For more information on **Charles Schulz**, please visit booklinks.abdopublishing.com

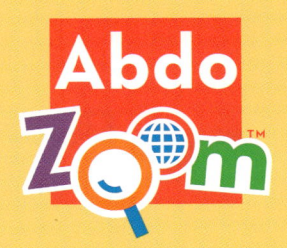

Zoom In on Biographies!

Learn even more with the Abdo Zoom Biographies database. Check out **abdozoom.com** for more information.

Index

born, 6

characters, 5, 7, 10, 14, 19

Charlie Brown, 5

comic strip, 4, 7, 9, 10, 12, 15, 16

died, 18

Li'l Folks, 10

Minnesota, 7

movies, 17

newspapers, 10, 12, 15

Peanuts, 4, 14, 16, 17, 18

school, 8

Snoopy, 5

TV, 17